D0535848

Ears

Injury, Illness and Health

Carol Ballard

Heinemann Library
Chicago, Illinois

Customer Service 888-454-2279

Visit our website at www.heinemannlibrary.com

Design: Jo Hinton-Malivoire and AMR
Illustrations: Art Construction

Originated by Blenheim Colour Ltd
Printed in China by Wing King Tong

07 06 05 04 03
10 9 8 7 6 5 4 3 2 1

Library of Congress Cataloging-in-Publication Data
Ballard, Carol.
    Ears / Carol Ballard.
        p. cm. -- (Body focus : injury, illness and health)
Includes bibliographical references and index.
Contents: Looking after your ears -- The outer ear -- Outer ear problems -- The middle ear -- Middle ear problems -- Inner ear -- Inner ear problems -- Balance : which way is up? -- Balance : moving around -- Motion sickness -- How do we hear? -- The cochlea -- Cochlear implants -- Different sounds -- Sounds all around -- Hearing tests and assessment -- Deafness -- Sign language -- Coping with deafness.
    ISBN: 1-4034-0749-5 (HC), ISBN 1-4034-3297-X (Pbk.)
    1. Ear--Juvenile literature. 2. Hearing--Juvenile literature. 3. Ear--Diseases--Juvenile literature. [1. Ear. 2. Hearing. 3. Senses and sensation.] I. Title. II. Series: Body focus.
    QP462.2.B347 2003
    612.8'5--dc21

                            2002152965

Acknowledgments
The author and publisher are grateful to the following for permission to reproduce copyright material:
pp. 6, 35 Alamy Images; p. 7 SPL/Malcolm Fielding, BOC Group; pp. 8 (left), 24, 25 Trip/H. Rogers; p. 8 (right) Creatas; p. 11 Actionplus; p. 13 SPL/CNRI; p. 14 SPL/Dr Kari Lountnaa; p. 15 SPL/Professor Tony Wright, Institute of Laryngology & Otology; pp. 18, 27 Getty Images; p. 19 AKG London; p. 21 Corbis/Royalty Free; p. 23 Popperfoto; p. 31 SPL/John Baosi; p. 36 SPL/CC Studio; p. 38 The Wellcome Photo Library; p. 39 SPL/BSIP Edmige; p. 41 SPL; p. 42 Leicester Mercury; p. 43 Arena.

Some words are shown in bold, **like this.** You can find out what they mean by looking in the glossary.

CONTENTS

INTRODUCTION

The ears are complex organs that allow you to hear a wide variety of different sounds. You can detect loud and soft sounds, from the roar of a jumbo jet taking off to the purring of a cat. You can detect high and low sounds, from the highest note of a piccolo to the lowest bass notes of a church organ. You can hear different qualities of sounds, such as the rumble of thunder, the crunching of dry leaves beneath your feet, and the electronic ring of a telephone. You can distinguish the tiniest differences in the sounds you hear, enabling you to know whose voice you are hearing, even when you cannot see the speaker. All of this information is very important to you. It helps you paint a picture of the world around you. Your ears also play an important role in helping you keep your balance.

Each ear has three main parts: the outer ear, the **middle ear,** and the **inner ear.**

Outer ear

The **pinna** is the part of the ear that you can see. This flap of skin and **cartilage** at the side of the head acts as a funnel for **sound waves.** It leads to the ear canal, a bony tube inside the head. A thin **membrane** called the **eardrum** sretches across the inner end of the ear canal.

Middle ear

The middle ear is a small space that contains three tiny bones called the **hammer,** the **anvil,** and the **stirrup.** Together these bones are called **ossicles.** At the end of the middle ear is another membrane, called the **oval window.** A short passage called the **eustachian tube** links the middle ear and the upper part of the throat.

Inner ear

Inside the inner ear, a complicated maze curls around and around in a bony spiral called the **cochlea.** Signals are transmitted from the cochlea to the brain by way of the **auditory nerve.** The **semicircular canals,** which control balance, are also part of the inner ear.

This diagram shows the structures of the outer, middle, and inner ears.

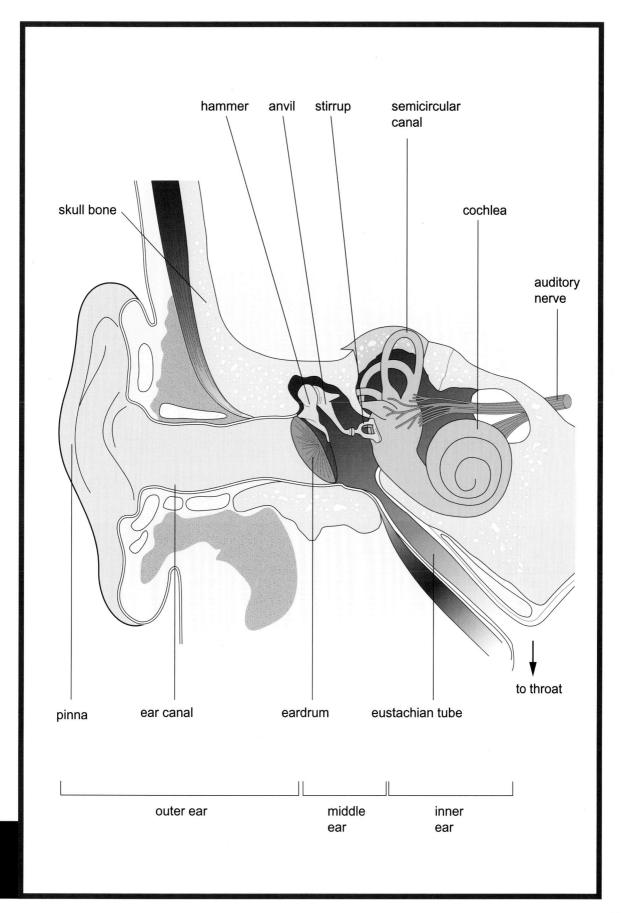

hammer anvil stirrup semicircular canal

cochlea

auditory nerve

skull bone

pinna ear canal eardrum eustachian tube

to throat

outer ear middle ear inner ear

5

TAKING CARE OF YOUR EARS

Your sense of hearing is very important. It allows you to react to sounds and interact with other people and the world around you. It is important to care for your ears and avoid damaging them.

Hygiene

You can keep your ears clean by washing them every day. Use either a warm, soapy washcloth or clean them under a shower. Never put anything in your ear to try to clean it. Your ear is very delicate, and you can easily cause irritation or damage.

Pierced ears

Many people like to have their earlobes pierced so that they can wear earrings. If you decide that you want this done, make sure that you choose a professional to do it. Piercing your own ears, or getting a friend to do it, often causes infection. After piercing, you need to keep your earrings in place until the holes are completely healed. During this time, keep the holes clean and free from infection by washing them with an antiseptic solution once or twice a day. If your ear becomes red, swollen, or painful, tell your parents or doctor right away. You may have an infection that will need treatment.

Many schools and sports teams only allow you to wear small stud earrings. This is for your own safety, because long, dangling earrings can get tugged or tangled, which can tear the earlobe. This is very painful!

Pierced ears may look attractive, but it is important to keep them clean so that they do not become infected.

Swimming

Whenever you swim, your ears are exposed to water that may not be very clean. It is a good idea to rinse your ears with clean water after you swim and then gently dry them. If your ears feel blocked, or you cannot hear properly after swimming, some water may be trapped in the ear canal. This is nothing to worry about. The water will usually just drain on its own.

Loud noises

Loud noises can damage the delicate structures of the ear and lead to deafness. You cannot protect your ears from all loud noises, but it makes sense to reduce those that you can.

Personal stereos and headphones can easily be turned up to levels that may seriously damage the ears. Read the instructions that come with your equipment and try to keep the volume low. If other people can hear your music, it is too loud for your ears.

Prolonged exposure to loud music at concerts and nightclubs can also lead to hearing problems. Some rock stars who have played very loud music for many years suffer from serious hearing loss. You can protect your ears by wearing earplugs. They won't keep you from hearing and enjoying the music, but they will reduce the likelihood of damage to your ears.

This engineer is wearing earmuffs to protect his ears from the loud noise of the machinery around him.

Ear protection
Ears can be protected from machinery noise or other loud sounds by wearing earmuffs or earplugs. It makes sense to wear these whenever you are in extremely noisy conditions.

The outer ear is made up of the **pinna,** the external auditory canal, and the **eardrum.**

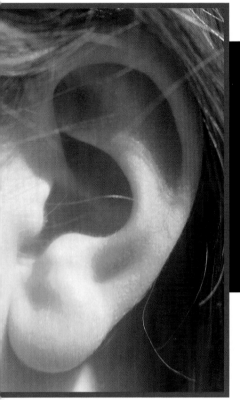

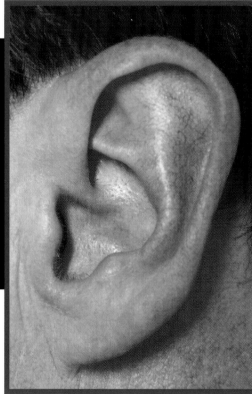

These two photographs show two common earlobe shapes. Look in a mirror at your own lobe shape, and then check out the rest of your family.

The pinna

The part of your ear that you can see at the side of your head is called the pinna. It is a flap of flexible **cartilage** covered with skin that is attached to your head with **ligaments** and muscles. Although different people have pinnae of different shapes and sizes, they all have the same basic structure. The curves of the pinna act as a funnel, collecting **sound waves** and channeling them into the ear canal.

Many animals are able to move their pinnae. Some can swivel them around to the direction of a sound to increase their level of hearing. Others use them to move air around, which helps them stay cool. Humans have lost the ability to move their pinnae, although some people can control the tiny muscles that allow them to wiggle just the tip of their earlobe.

Earlobes come in one of two basic shapes. They have either a gentle curve away from the side of the head, or they dip down and up again. These shapes tend to run in families and are inherited in a way similar to eye and hair color.

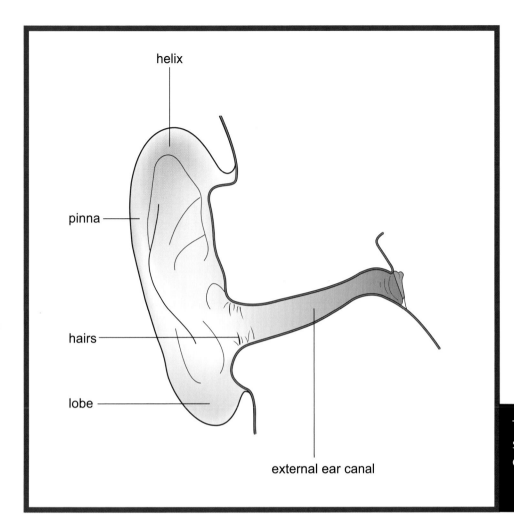

helix

pinna

hairs

lobe

external ear canal

This diagram shows the outer ear.

External ear canal

The narrow external ear canal is a tube that is 0.79 to 1.18 inches (2 to 3 centimeters) long. It stretches from the pinna to the eardrum. The outer third of the ear canal is made of flexible cartilage, and the rest is channeled out of the bones of the skull. The external ear canal helps protect the eardrum from changes in temperature and humidity.

The cartilage and bone of the ear canal are covered with skin. Fine hairs grow from the skin, pointing outward toward the pinna. Special glands in the skin produce cerumen, or earwax. Earwax helps keep the skin of the ear canal moist. It also traps dead skin, dust, and **bacteria.** Together with the hairs, earwax helps prevent dirt from reaching the eardrum. Earwax usually dries up and falls out of the ear canal.

Eardrum
The eardrum, or tympanic **membrane,** is a thin see-through barrier between the outer ear and the **middle ear.** It is a fine sheet of fibrous tissue made up of layers of circular and **radial fibers** that give it elasticity. The eardrum contains many tiny blood vessels and nerve endings. This is why damage to the eardrum may cause bleeding and pain.

Getting stuck!

The golden rule is to never put anything into your ears. It is amazingly easy for things to get stuck in them! Very young children sometimes put small toys or other objects in their ears. They may be just finding out about their bodies, or they may be playing and not realize the danger of what they are doing. Often, a doctor is needed to remove the object. Adults cleaning their ears with cotton swabs or twists of tissue may also end up with a piece stuck in the ear canal and find that they, too, cannot remove it without help.

Too much wax

Earwax usually dries up and is pushed outward along the ear canal by tiny hairs. It eventually falls out on its own. Some people, especially those with very dusty jobs, produce a lot of earwax. It may build up in the ear canal, causing irritation, noises in the ear, and dulled hearing. Attempts to remove it with cotton swabs often only push it in even farther. A doctor can easily remove excess wax by softening it, often with a few drops of warm olive oil. He or she then uses a jet of warm water and a syringe to suck the wax out. The ear can then be cleaned and dried, and hearing should be normal again. This process may not sound pleasant, but cleaning the ears in this way should not hurt at all.

Infections

The outer ear can become infected by **bacteria.** If this happens, a sticky liquid may ooze from the ear. If the liquid blocks the ear canal, the person may also experience some hearing loss in the infected ear.

Infections can easily be treated with **antibiotics**, either as tablets or as eardrops. As the infection clears, the person's hearing returns to normal.

Cauliflower ears

Some sports can cause frequent **abrasion** and rubbing of the **pinna**, resulting in the damage known as cauliflower ear. Many players protect their ears with a helmet or other headgear, such as the ear guards used in wrestling. Other athletes may tape their ears flat to the head to avoid damage. If you play a sport where your ears may be damaged, it is important to do all you can to protect them.

This rugby player's ears are badly damaged after years of abrasion and rubbing. The lumpy appearance is typical of cauliflower ear. Many players wear protective headgear to prevent this type of damage.

THE MIDDLE EAR

As its name suggests, the **middle ear** lies between the outer ear and the **inner ear.** It is a small space within the skull bones and contains the **ossicles,** the smallest bones in the human body.

The middle ear has a narrow, irregular shape that is filled with air. It is separated from the ear canal by the **eardrum.** Two further **membranes,** the **oval window** and the **round window,** separate the middle ear from the inner ear.

Eustachian tube

The **eustachian tube,** also called the auditory tube, forms a link between the middle ear and the back of the upper mouth. The main purpose of the eustachian tube is to keep the air pressure inside the middle ear the same as the air pressure in the ear canal. If the difference in pressure is too great, the eardrum may be distorted. The eustachian tube maintains the balance of pressure by allowing air from the nasal cavity to pass into the middle ear. The eustachian tube stays closed while there is a balance of pressure. If the outside pressure is greater than the inside pressure, the eustachian tube opens, allowing air to flow from the nose into the middle ear. You have probably felt your ears pop as the pressure inside adjusts at some time, perhaps in a car going uphill or on a carnival ride.

This diagram shows the structures inside the middle ear.

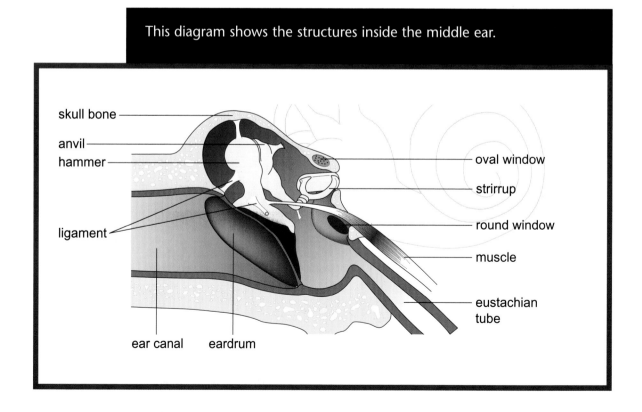

skull bone

anvil

hammer

ligament

oval window

stirrup

round window

muscle

eustachian tube

ear canal   eardrum

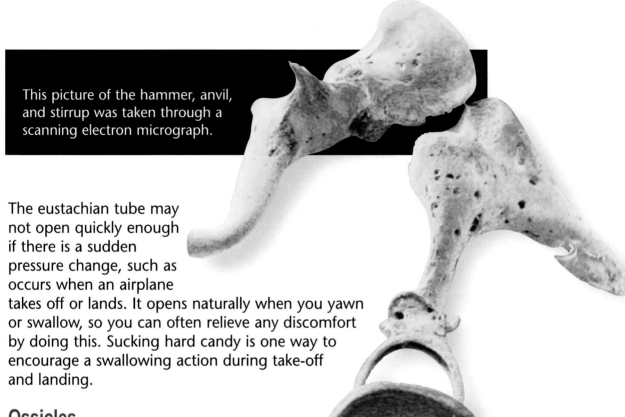

This picture of the hammer, anvil, and stirrup was taken through a scanning electron micrograph.

The eustachian tube may not open quickly enough if there is a sudden pressure change, such as occurs when an airplane takes off or lands. It opens naturally when you yawn or swallow, so you can often relieve any discomfort by doing this. Sucking hard candy is one way to encourage a swallowing action during take-off and landing.

Ossicles

The ossicles are three tiny, intricately shaped bones that lie inside the middle ear. They fit together very accurately and are held in place by **ligaments** attached to the inside of the middle ear. They form a chain of levers between the eardrum and the oval window. The names of the ossicles come from their shapes and movements: the **hammer, anvil,** and **stirrup.** The handle (the thinner end) of the hammer touches the eardrum, and the head (the wider end) of the hammer is linked to the anvil. The anvil is linked to the stirrup, and the base of the stirrup touches the oval window.

Two tiny, delicate muscles control the movements of the ossicles. One is attached to the head of the hammer. It limits the size of its movements, protecting the middle ear from very loud noises. The other is attached to the neck of the stirrup. It limits its movement. This protects the oval window, but makes your hearing less sensitive.

Loud noises

Although the muscles respond very quickly when there is a sudden loud sound, they cannot contract instantly. They can protect the ears from continuous loud noises, such as machinery, but they cannot respond quickly enough to protect the ears from very sudden, short noises, such as a gunshot.

MIDDLE EAR PROBLEMS

Otitis media

Otitis media is the medical term for a **middle ear** infection. It usually follows a sore throat or cold, when **viruses** and **bacteria** may travel to the middle ear by way of the **eustachian tube.** The middle ear becomes inflamed and extremely painful. Pus is produced and, because it cannot drain, the pressure inside the middle ear increases. Ringing noises and other sounds may be heard inside the ear, and hearing is reduced. The **eardrum** becomes red and bulges outward. In severe cases, the eardrum may even burst, allowing pus to drain out of the ear canal. Usually the infection is treated with **antibiotics,** which prevent the condition from reaching this level of severity. When the infection clears, hearing returns to normal.

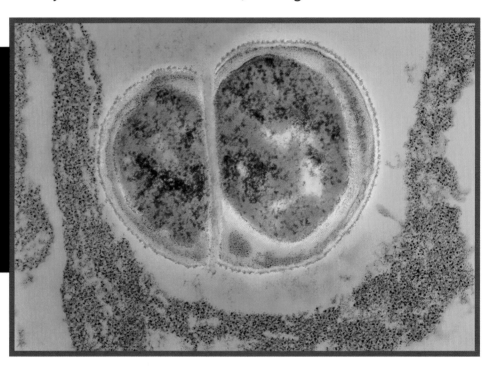

This photograph is of a culture of *Alloiococcus otitidis*, a bacterium that is responsible for many middle ear infections.

Glue ear

Glue ear affects one in ten children at some time during childhood. It is the result of chronic inflammation of the middle ear, possibly caused by persistent infections or allergies. The eustachian tube does not work properly, so air cannot reach the middle ear. Thick fluid builds up inside the middle ear and keeps the **ossicles** from moving freely. The child gradually loses his or her hearing. Treatment is usually with **decongestant** medicine. In some cases, however, a minor operation is necessary. Fluid can be drained by making a tiny hole in the eardrum. A small plastic tube called a grommet is put into the hole, allowing air to reach the middle ear. The ear can then slowly return to normal. As the eardrum grows, the grommet is slowly pushed out.

Although glue ear is not dangerous and does not cause long-term hearing loss, it is important to detect it as soon as possible. Hearing plays a vital role in the learning process, and if a child's hearing is reduced for a while, his or her education is likely to suffer.

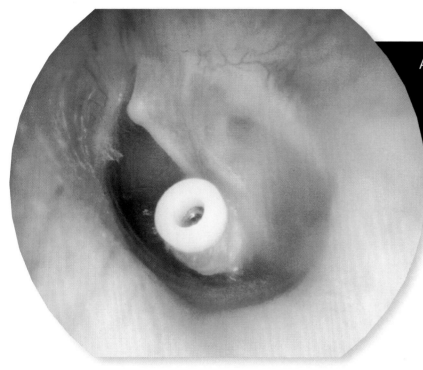

A grommet such as this one may be inserted into a hole in the eardrum if a child is suffering from glue ear.

Otosclerosis

Otosclerosis is a rare condition. It usually occurs in teenagers and young adults. It affects more women than men, and scientists believe there may be a **genetic** cause, as it tends to run in families. The ability of the ossicles to transmit vibrations gradually decreases as extra bone material is produced around the **stirrup.** The ossicles become stiff, and hearing is slowly reduced, resulting eventually in deafness.

Several types of treatment are available. The faulty stirrup may be removed, and a plastic one inserted in its place. Surgery may be carried out to reduce the amount of extra bone around the stirrup, restoring its freedom of movement. Hearing aids have been developed to bypass the ossicles. They transmit **sound waves** to the **inner ear** by way of the skull bones.

Cholesteatoma

Cholesteatoma is a rare condition in which a cyst, or fluid-filled lump, develops inside the middle ear. It causes pain, fluid discharge, and hearing loss. As the cyst grows, it destroys the surrounding bone and may also destroy the eardrum and bones of the middle ear. The cyst can be surgically removed, but it may take several operations to remove it entirely.

THE INNER EAR

The **inner ear** lies within the bones of the skull, safe from injury and damage. Unlike the outer ear and **middle ear,** the inner ear is filled with fluid. It contains the last part of the chain of structures that make hearing possible. And it contains the sensitive organs that help the body maintain its sense of balance. The inner ear is also called the labyrinth, because its spiral structure of canals is similar to a maze.

The bones of the skull are hollowed out, creating a bony space lined with a thin **membrane.** The central area of this space is called the vestibule. It is separated from the middle ear by the **oval window.**

There are two main parts of the inner ear:
• the organs concerned with balance: the **semicircular canals, utriculus,** and **saccule** (see pages 20–23)
• the spiral **cochlea,** which is concerned with hearing.

The semicircular canals are sensitive to rotational movements of the head. There are three semicircular canals, two vertical and one horizontal. They are arranged at right angles to each other, like three sides of a cube. Each detects tiny movements of the head in one direction and sends signals to the brain, providing information about the speed and direction of the movement.

The utriculus and saccule are sensitive to changes of posture. They send signals to the brain, which provide information when the head tilts from side to side or tips backward and forward.

Together, these structures allow the brain to pinpoint precisely the movements and position of the head.

This diagram shows the structures of the inner ear.

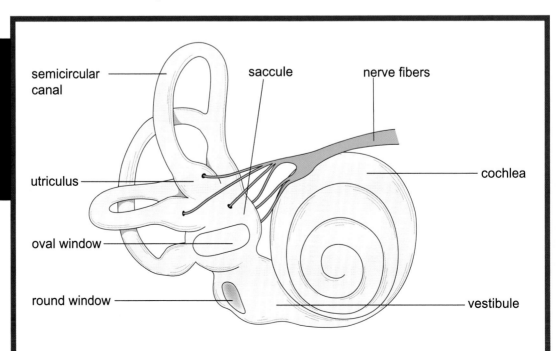

semicircular canal

saccule

nerve fibers

utriculus

cochlea

oval window

round window

vestibule

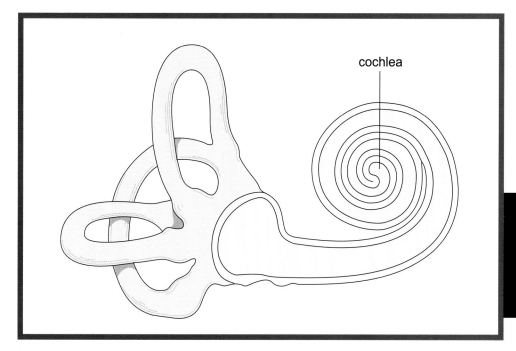

cochlea

The cochlea spirals around more than two and a half times.

Cochlea

The cochlea gets its name from the Greek word for snail, *kokhlos*, because it spirals around like a snail's shell. It is a bony tube that winds around itself a little more than two and a half times. The cochlea has a central bony core, and three ducts run parallel along its length, just as wires run together along a length of electrical cable. Each duct is separated from the others by a membrane.

The central duct contains the **spiral organ.** This is what allows you to hear sounds. It has a complicated arrangement of **hair cells,** each with bristle-like sensory hairs. Each hair cell is linked to nerve fibers, and these join larger bundles of nerves to carry signals from the cochlea to the auditory area of the brain.

The base of the cochlea is separated from the middle ear by another membrane, which covers a bony hole called the **round window.**

Discovery of the cochlea

In 1561, an Italian professor named Gabriello Fallopio discovered the cochlea, although he mistakenly thought that it was filled with air. It was nearly 300 years later, in 1851, that improved microscopes allowed another Italian scientist, Alfonso Corti, to examine the structure of the inner ear more closely. He discovered that the cochlea was filled with liquid. He was even able to see the tiny hair cells. For many years, the spiral organ was known as the organ of Corti.

Inner ear problems can be the result of the **cochlea** not functioning properly or a failure of the **auditory nerve** to carry signals to the brain. These problems can be caused by reduced blood flow to the ears due to narrowing of the arteries, exposure to loud noises, or head injury. They can also be caused by some drugs and some diseases, including mumps and meningitis. If a pregnant woman catches rubella, or German measles, it can cause serious damage to her baby's ears.

Ménières disease

Ménières disease is caused by excess fluid in the inner ear, which increases the pressure inside. A person with this condition usually has bad attacks of vertigo, or dizziness, and a feeling of sickness, together with hearing loss. The ears may feel full and as though they are about to burst. The person may also hear roaring and hissing sounds. Attacks may last just a few minutes or several hours. After each attack, everything slowly returns to normal, although over a period of time, the person's hearing gradually worsens. Some drugs can help reduce the symptoms, and in some cases, an operation to drain the excess fluid can help. In other cases, special hearing aids can help but may not solve the problem completely.

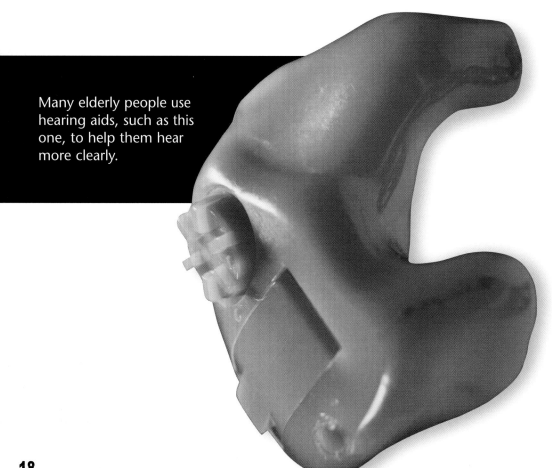

Many elderly people use hearing aids, such as this one, to help them hear more clearly.

Labyrinthitis

Labyrinthitis is inflammation of the inner ear, usually caused by a **bacterial** or **viral** infection, allergies, or toxic drugs. The person feels dizzy and sick and suffers a hearing loss. He or she often falls over, in the direction of the affected ear. Labyrinthitis can usually be treated successfully with drugs, with no permanent hearing loss.

Tinnitus

Tinnitus is the name given to the condition in which a person hears ringing or buzzing noises that do not actually exist. It is not really one single problem but can be the result of several different problems. It can be caused by outer ear problems, such as earwax stuck in the ear canal, and by **middle ear** problems, such as infections. In most cases, however, it arises as a result of damage to the cochlea. Although some drugs may help a little, tinnitus is difficult to treat. Some patients wear a masking device, a small piece of equipment that fits into the ear like a hearing aid. The device produces a constant noise that takes the patient's attention away from the irritating tinnitus sounds.

Beethoven suffered from the ringing and roaring sounds of tinnitus for many years.

Presbyacusis

As people age, their sense of hearing slowly deteriorates because **hair cells** in the cochlea are gradually lost. This process is called presbyacusis. The ability to hear high-**frequency** sounds is usually lost before the ability to hear low-frequency sounds. Elderly people can often hear a mumbling noise when people speak to them but are unable to distinguish words clearly. Hearing aids can amplify, or increase, the frequencies that a person cannot detect, allowing him or her to hear more clearly again.

The **inner ear** plays an important part in helping you keep your balance. The **utriculus** and **saccule** both help your body know instinctively which way is up. They are also involved in the detection of sudden head movements.

The walls of the utriculus and saccule each contain a small area that is thicker than the rest. These are called the maculae (one is a macula), and they are perpendicular to each other. They contain the receptors that collect information about the position of the head, allowing you to keep your balance.

Each macula contains **hair cells** and supporting cells. Each hair cell is linked to nerve fibers. A jellylike layer, called the **otolithic membrane**, lies on top of the hair cells. The surface of this membrane is covered by a layer of granules, called **otoliths.**

Forward and backward

When you tilt your head forward, gravity pulls the otolithic membrane and the otoliths. This makes them slide over the hair cells. As they slide, they bend the hair cells, and the hair cells respond by sending signals to the brain. When the brain receives signals, it interprets the information about the direction in which the head is tilted.

When you tilt your head backward, the otolithic membrane and otoliths are pulled in the opposite direction, and the hair cells are bent in the opposite direction.

Because it depends on gravity and does not rely on information from the eyes, this system should work without any visual signals. Most of the time it does. For example, when you are underwater or in complete darkness, you can still tell which way is up. The system does not always work, however. It is not unknown for an airplane pilot to fly upside down in dense clouds and not even realize it!

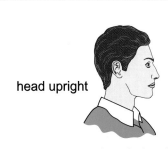
head upright

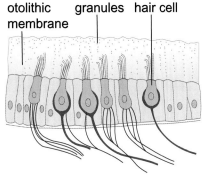
otolithic membrane   granules   hair cell

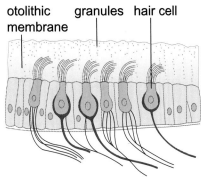
head tilted forward

otolithic membrane   granules   hair cell

These diagrams show how the hair cells in the macula are bent when the head is tilted forward.

In space

Astronauts find it difficult to tell which way is up. The utriculus and saccule rely on the pull of gravity to move the otolithic membrane and otoliths. In the zero gravity of space, there is no pull, and so this mechanism does not work.

Somersault!

You spend most of your waking life with your head upright. In some sports, however, people turn upside down rapidly over and over again. Imagine what must be happening inside the inner ears of a gymnast or diver who turns one somersault after another!

Gymnasts rely on their sense of balance for many of their intricate moves.

BALANCE: MOVING AROUND

Whether you are moving or standing still, you need to maintain your balance. Movements of the head are detected by the **semicircular canals** in the **inner ear,** and this information is passed to the brain for processing and action.

The inner ear contains three semicircular canals set at right angles to each other, like three sides of a cube. They respond to turning and rotating movements of the head.

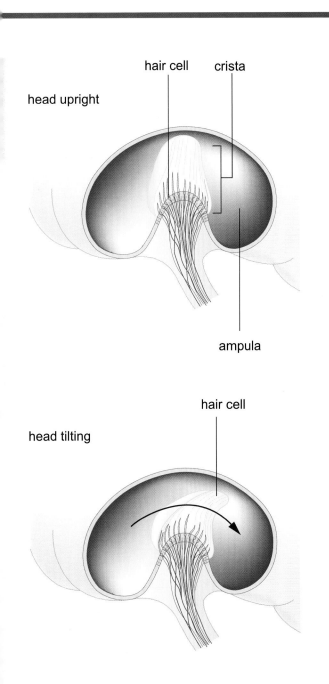

hair cell   crista

head upright

ampula

hair cell

head tilting

Semicircular canal

Each semicircular canal is filled with fluid. In each canal is a bulge called an ampulla. Inside each ampulla is a raised area called the crista. The crista has a patch of **hair cells** and supporting cells. The hair cells stick out into a jellylike flap called a cupula. The mechanism works similar to a hinged door. The crista is the door frame and hinge, and the cupula is free to swing back and forth like a door opening and closing. As the cupula moves, its free edge brushes against the curved wall of the ampulla. When the head rotates, the fluid in the semicircular canal lags behind, pushing the cupula and bending the hair cells. As they bend, the hair cells send signals to the brain. The brain processes the information about the direction in which the head is moving.

The semicircular canals can detect only quick, jerky movements. This is because during slow, steady movements, the fluid inside the canals does not lag behind.

These diagrams show how the hair cells of the semicircular canals are bent when the head rotates.

Feeling dizzy

If you spin around and around quickly, you often feel dizzy when you stop. This is because the fluid in the semicircular canals keeps moving for a while, even when your head is still, so it continues to bend the hair cells. You know you are not moving, but your brain is still receiving signals from the inner ear telling it that you are moving. You feel dizzy. You may feel as though you are still moving, but in the opposite direction to that in which you were spinning. Or you may feel that you are still, and that everything around you is moving.

The inner ear of people who are deaf often does not function at all, so they never feel dizzy!

The semicircular canals do not rely on the pull of gravity, so they work in zero gravity. Therefore, astronauts have no problem detecting their head movements.

Ice-skaters fix their eyes on one spot to avoid feeling dizzy when they stop spinning.

Dizziness

The feeling of dizziness can be a problem for people who spin around a lot, such as ice-skaters and ballet dancers. To pirouette, they train themselves to keep their eyes fixed on one spot, so that with each spin their eyes go back to that spot. This helps them avoid feeling dizzy when they stop.

MOTION SICKNESS

Chances are you have experienced motion sickness. You may feel sick traveling in a car or a bus or on a rough sea in a boat. You get this sensation when the messages sent to the brain from the eyes do not agree with those from the ears. Other factors may be involved as well.

Symptoms

Some people suffer from motion sickness no matter how they travel. Others may suffer in only one particular form of transportation. Motion sickness usually causes a person to look pale and feel sick. Many people suffer a cold sweat and vomit.

Motion sickness occurs when the brain receives two different signals from the eyes and **inner ears.** For example, if you are a passenger in a car, your inner ears detect no movement because the forward movement of the car is steady, but your eyes detect the movement of the scenery passing by. The brain receives signals from the ears telling it you are not moving, but signals from the eyes tell it you *are* moving. Putting these two together can cause a problem—and you sometimes feel sick.

The opposite happens if you are in a windowless room within a boat. Your ears detect the rocking movement of the boat, but your eyes detect no movement in your surroundings. Again, the brain receives different signals, and you may feel sick.

Carnival rides that spin you around can make you feel dizzy and sick.

Other factors are involved in motion sickness. If you have had motion sickness before, you may unknowingly expect to be sick again, and this expectation can make you feel sick. Psychologists call this a conditioned reflex.

How to avoid it

To avoid motion sickness, you need to try to match the two sets of signals as much as you can. In a car, looking out of a window will lessen the visual movement. In a boat, looking at the horizon will balance the actual movement and the visual movement.

Children between the ages of four and twelve are most likely to suffer from motion sickness, although many children never experience it at all. Many people slowly adjust, and by the time they are teenagers, they know what they should avoid. For example, reading in a car can make many people feel sick. Some people, however, are not able to adjust and may suffer from motion sickness all their lives.

These wristbands press on special points and may help to prevent motion sickness.

Remedies for motion sickness

Drugs are available to help combat motion sickness. Some work by suppressing the balance system, and others work by suppressing vomiting. These drugs can cause drowsiness or sleepiness, and many people prefer to rely on drug-free remedies. These include flexible wristbands that press on certain points and herbal remedies such as eating ginger. Avoiding heavy meals, especially fatty, fried foods, can help reduce the feelings of sickness. Fresh air is important, too, because stuffy air can lead to sleepiness and sickness.

HOW DO YOU HEAR?

When a sound is made, vibrations spread out in all directions from the source of the sound. These vibrations, called **sound waves**, travel through the air. You hear the sound when these vibrations enter your ears.

This diagram shows how vibrations from a sound wave travel through the ear. The numbers on the diagram correspond to the numbers in the text.

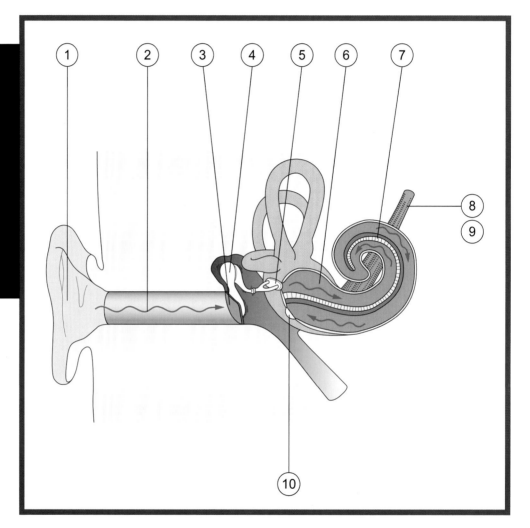

The outer ear, **middle ear,** and **inner ear** all play a part in allowing you to hear sounds. When a sound wave enters your ear, a rapid sequence of events begins that results in your hearing the sound.

1. The **pinna** acts as a funnel, channeling sound waves into the ear canal.
2. Sound waves travel inward along the ear canal.
3. When the sound waves reach the **eardrum,** they make it vibrate.
4. As the eardrum vibrates backward and forward, it makes the **hammer** vibrate. This makes the **anvil** vibrate, which, in turn, makes the **stirrup** vibrate.
5. The vibrations of the stirrup make the **oval window** vibrate.

6. The vibrations of the oval window cause the fluid in the **cochlea** to vibrate.
7. As the fluid vibrates, it bends some of the **hair cells** of the cochlea.
8. The hair cells that are bent send electrical signals to the brain by way of the **auditory nerve.**
9. The brain receives the signals and processes the information. You hear the sound.
10. Pressure waves travel to the **round window,** making it bulge outward. The waves are lost as the pressure passes into the middle ear and is equalized by the **eustachian tube.**

Different ear models

Different mammals' ears may be different shapes, but they all have the same basic structure. Other animals have very different ears. Some creatures have no outer ear, but their eardrum is on the surface of the body, with a simplified internal system. This arrangement is called a tympanal organ. In frogs, the tympanal organs are on the side of the head. In other creatures, such as crickets, they are on the legs.

Sound waves travel through the air away from the sound source, just as these ripples travel away from a stone dropped into a pond.

THE COCHLEA

The **cochlea** is a coiled structure within the **inner ear.** It responds to the vibrations of **sound waves** by transmitting electrical signals to the brain.

As the diagram on page 17 shows, the cochlea is a bony spiral. Inside the central duct of this spiral is the **spiral organ.** This is a coiled sheet of cells, which includes **hair cells** and supporting cells. The hair cells are connected to nerve cells.

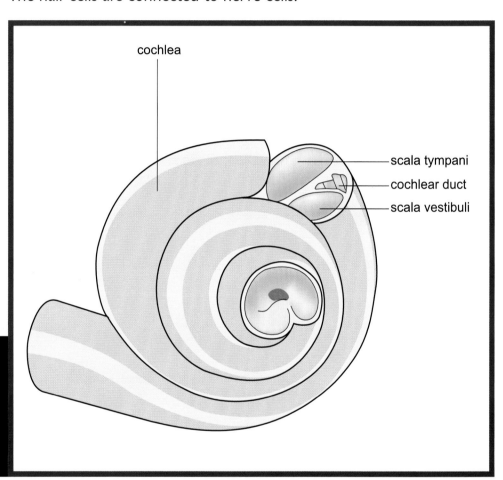

cochlea

scala tympani
cochlear duct
scala vestibuli

In this diagram, you can see the structure of the bony spiral of the cochlea.

Hair cells

There are two groups of hair cells: inner hair cells and outer hair cells. Inner hair cells are arranged in a single row that extends along the whole length of the cochlea. More than 90 percent of these cells are connected to nerve cells that carry information to the brain.

Outer hair cells are arranged in three rows. Most of these cells are also connected to nerve cells. On each hair cell, the hairs are arranged in the pattern of a *U* or a *W.* The tip of each hair cell is embedded in a jellylike layer, the **tectorial membrane.**

How does the cochlea work?

When a sound wave reaches the outer ear, it is transmitted through the **middle ear.** Eventually the vibrations reach the inner ear. Pressure waves are created in the fluid in the cochlea, and these waves make the **basilar membrane** vibrate. This makes the hair cells move. As they move, they brush against the tectorial membrane and their tips are bent. They respond to this bending by sending signals along the nerve cells to which they are connected.

This diagram shows the cells that make up the spiral organ.

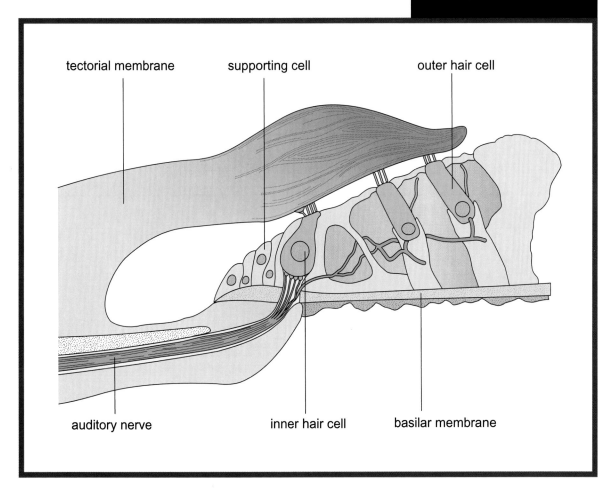

tectorial membrane   supporting cell   outer hair cell

auditory nerve   inner hair cell   basilar membrane

Making sounds

Amazingly, the cochlea itself can also produce sounds! As the outer hair cells move, they cause vibrations that can be detected by a doctor placing a very sensitive microphone next to the **eardrum.** These sounds can be useful in the detection of hearing defects in newborn babies. If no sounds are produced, it shows that the outer hair cells are not moving and the cochlea is not responding to vibrations.

COCHLEAR IMPLANTS

Cochlear implants can be used to restore some hearing in people whose **cochleas** are not functioning properly. These small electronic devices bypass the cochlea and send tiny electrical signals directly to the brain.

What is a cochlear implant?

Cochlear implants are made up of five parts: a small microphone worn behind the ear; a speech processor that fits in a pocket; a transmitting coil behind the ear; a receiver/stimulator implanted behind the ear; and an electrode array implanted into the cochlea.

The technology involved in cochlear implants is continually advancing. Devices are likely to get smaller and work more efficiently as designs become increasingly sophisticated.

Cochlear implants do not yet provide a normal standard of hearing, but most people with implants are able to hear medium and loud sounds. Some are able to hear well enough to be able to use the telephone, which they would be unable to do without the implant.

How does an implant work?

1. The microphone detects a sound and sends it to the speech processor.
2. The speech processor amplifies and filters the sound and turns it into electrical signals that it sends to the transmitting coil.
3. The transmitting coil passes the signals to the receiver/stimulator.
4. The receiver/stimulator stimulates electrodes in the electrode array.
5. The electrodes stimulate the **auditory nerve.**
6. The auditory nerve transmits the signals to the auditory center in the brain, as in normal hearing.
7. The person hears the sound.

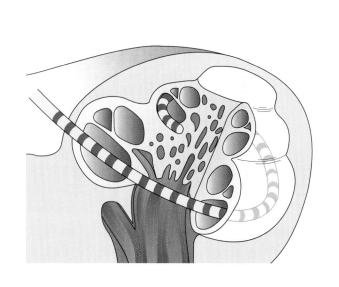

This diagram shows how the electrode array (shown here as the red and yellow striped tube) coils around inside the cochlea.

How does a patient receive an implant?

Cochlear implants are placed using surgery. The operation usually takes a couple of hours. A small cut is made in the skin just behind the ear, and the receiver/stimulator is placed against the skull bone. A tiny hole is drilled in the skull bone, allowing an even tinier hole to be drilled in the cochlea. The electrode array is then gently inserted into the cochlea through this hole. The wound is stitched and given time to heal. After a few weeks, the other parts of the implant can be fitted, and an **audiologist** makes sure that the sound level is comfortable for the person. Regular checkups are necessary to ensure that the settings are right and that the implant is working properly.

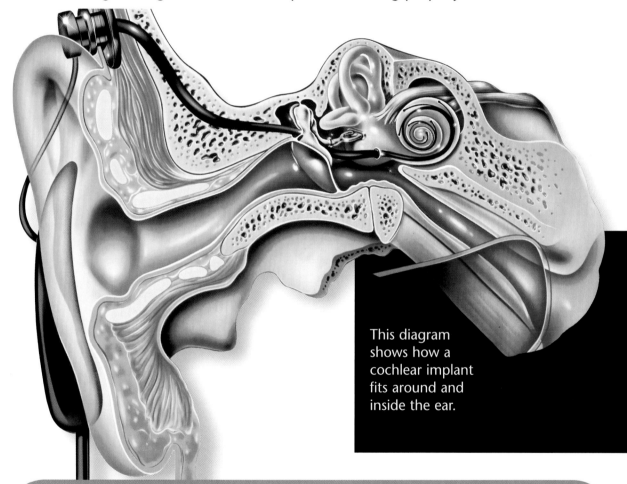

This diagram shows how a cochlear implant fits around and inside the ear.

Living with a cochlear implant

People who have been deaf for a long time need a while to get used to hearing sounds again. They may need support and help to enable them to communicate effectively. Children who have never heard any sound at all can react in a variety of ways. Some are surprised, some are happy, and others are puzzled.

DIFFERENT SOUNDS

The human ear can detect a wide variety of differences among sounds, such as whether they are high or low, loud or soft. It can also detect differences in the quality of a sound and can often tell what has made the sound. For example, you can tell whether a sound is made by metal hitting metal or wood hitting wood.

High and low

Pitch is a term that describes how high or low a sound is. The pitch of a sound depends on the speed of the vibrations. The faster the vibrations, the higher the pitch. The speed of the vibrations is called the **frequency** and is measured in Hertz (Hz): 1 Hz = 1 cycle per second. Human ears can usually hear sounds that vibrate between 20 and 20,000 times every second (20 Hz and 20,000 Hz). Human speech usually contains sounds between 100 and 3,000 Hz. Some animals, such as dogs and bats, can hear very high frequency sounds that human ears cannot pick up.

Detecting pitch

You can detect differences in pitch because each part of the **cochlea** responds to a different frequency of vibration. High-pitch sounds, with fast vibrations, are detected by the part of the cochlea closest to the **oval window.** Low-pitch sounds, with slow vibrations, are detected by the other end of the cochlea. When the brain receives the signal by way of the **auditory nerve,** it knows which part of the cochlea has responded to the sound. Therefore, it knows what the pitch of the sound must be.

These oscilloscope screens show the patterns of different sound waves:
a. very fast vibrations—high-pitched sound
b. very slow vibrations—low-pitched sound
c. very big vibrations—loud sound
d. very small vibrations—soft sound
e. a recorder playing middle C
f. a woman singing middle C

In (e) and (f), the notes have the same pitch and volume, but the wave patterns are different because the mixtures of noises are different.

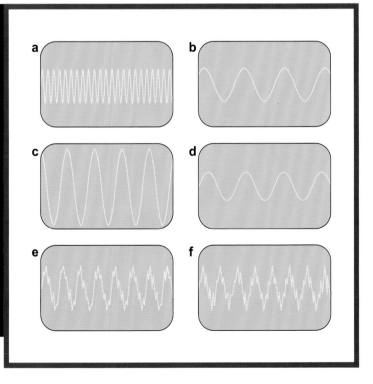

Loud and soft

The loudness of a sound as it reaches your **eardrum** is called the volume. The intensity of a sound is the amount of energy in the **sound waves**. If you are a long way from a high-intensity sound, its volume may be less than that of a low-intensity sound that is close to you. Intensity is measured in decibels (dB). The quietest sound that can be detected by a normal human ear is 0 dB and is called the threshold of hearing. The table below shows the intensity of some everyday sounds.

sound	intensity
whispering	30 db
normal conversation	60 dB
shouting/screaming	80 dB
thunder	100 dB
airplane taking off	120 dB

You can detect differences in the volume of sounds because of differences in the sizes of the vibrations. The louder the sound, the bigger the vibration. Bigger vibrations stimulate more **hair cells**, so more signals are sent to the brain. The brain processes the information, knowing that the more signals it receives, the louder the sound must be.

Quality of sound

Few sounds are pure. Most are made up of a mixture of noises. You can compare sound to color. Red, blue, and yellow are primary—or pure—colors, but they can be mixed together in different proportions to produce all the colors of the rainbow. Sounds are similar. Each is made up of a distinctive mixture of high and low, loud and soft components, mixed together to form a huge range of sounds. The brain recognizes each specific mixture it receives by way of the cochlea and identifies the sound.

When you hear a sound, you can often tell from which direction it came. This is because you have two ears, positioned on opposite sides of the head. Each ear receives a slightly different sound and passes a slightly different signal to the brain.

Sound waves

When a sound is made, **sound waves** travel through the air. Unless the sound source is directly in front, behind, or above you, one ear will be closer to the sound source than the other. The sound waves will reach the closer ear before they reach the other ear. For this reason, signals from the closer ear reach the brain before signals from the other ear. This difference is only a tiny fraction of a second! However, the brain can detect the difference and can use the information to pinpoint the direction of the sound.

As the sound waves travel away from the sound source, the vibrations gradually get smaller, just as ripples in a pond get smaller as they spread out from a stone dropped into the water. This means that the farther away from the sound source you are, the quieter the sound will be. The ear that is closer to the sound source will receive slightly bigger vibrations than the other ear. More **hair cells** will be stimulated in the closer ear than in the other ear. The brain can detect this difference, and this information helps it to pinpoint the direction of the sound.

The ear closer to the sound source receives the vibration a fraction of a second before the other ear does.

The ear closer to the sound source hears a slightly louder sound than the other ear hears.

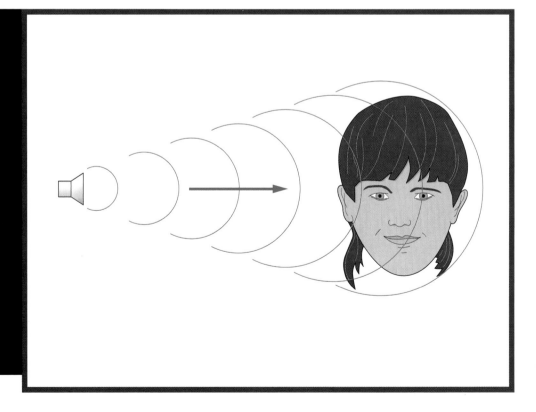

Moving ears

Most mammals can move their ear **pinnae** to help them locate the direction of a sound. Humans cannot do this. Instead, you must move your head.

To locate sounds, humans rely on signals from each ear reaching the brain. So people who are deaf in one ear find it almost impossible to locate the direction of a sound.

Stereo sound systems

Most people enjoy listening to music of some sort. Early radios and record players used a mono system. All the sound came from the same direction, from a single speaker. This gave an artificial sound and could not reproduce the sounds as they would have been heard live. As technology advanced, stereo systems were developed. Sounds were recorded from left and right positions and fed to left and right speakers. By placing the two speakers at each side of a room, a much more accurate reproduction of the sound could be achieved. Personal stereo sound systems send a different sound directly to each ear by way of headphones. Modern technology is introducing new systems all the time, with quadrophonic sound (four speakers) and more.

A dog can locate a sound in 1 of 32 positions, while a human can locate it in only 1 of 8 positions.

Accurate animals

Many animals are able to locate sounds more accurately than humans. A cat can accurately locate two sounds 1.6 feet (.5 meter) apart at a distance of 59 feet (18 meters). A dog is able to pinpoint the direction of a sound very accurately indeed. Imagine a circle divided into 32 equal segments. A dog can locate exactly which segment a sound comes from. A human's hearing is much less accurate. You cannot pinpoint a sound more accurately than one-eighth of the circle, in other words, four of the dog's segments put together.

HEARING TESTS

Hearing is a complex sense. Therefore, assessment of a person's hearing requires several different tests. Routine hearing tests can be carried out as part of a general health checkup by a family doctor, but if a problem is suspected, special tests can be carried out by an **audiologist.**

Physical examination

Doctors examine the ear using an otoscope. This is an instrument that contains a light and a magnifying lens. It allows the doctor to see the ear canal and **eardrum.** During a physical examination, a doctor checks for excess wax, foreign objects, eardrum damage, and signs of infection. This examination may clearly show the cause of any hearing loss, and the doctor can prescribe appropriate treatment. If the doctor can find no reason for a hearing loss, the patient may be referred to an audiologist for special tests.

This doctor is using an otoscope to examine the patient's ear.

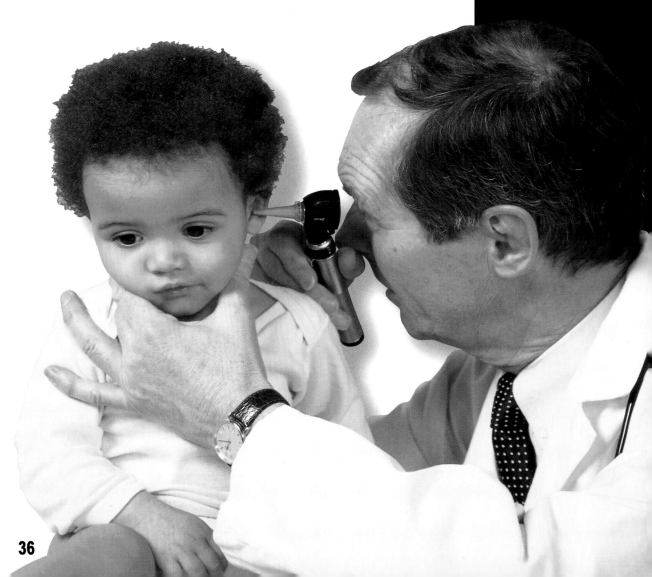

Audiologist assessment

Audiologists try to find the extent and cause of hearing loss. Tests can show the **frequency** range and levels of intensity of sounds that a patient can hear. Tests can distinguish among problems in the outer ear, **middle ear,** and **inner ear.** The results can be used to suggest treatment and ensure that, if a hearing aid is used, it is adjusted correctly.

Testing the outer ear

There are three ways to test the outer ear:

- Pure tone test. This test is carried out in a soundproof room to cut out any background noise. Sounds of different **pitches** and intensities are introduced to a person by way of speakers or headphones, and the person indicates when he or she has heard a sound. Responses are recorded on a chart called an audiogram.
- Speech audiometry. This test estimates the lowest level at which a person can hear speech.
- Word recognition. This tests how well a person understands what he or she hears.

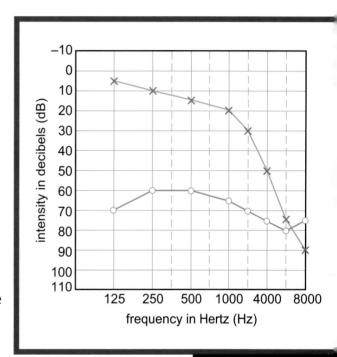

Testing the middle ear

To test how well the middle ear conducts **sound waves** to the inner ear, an audiologist gently increases the air pressure in the ear canal and measures the movement of the eardrum in response to different sounds. The results are shown on a chart called a tympanogram.

Testing the inner ear

The bones of the skull can conduct sounds and can be used to test the inner ear. A special headset is placed on the bone behind the ear, and the person is asked to respond to sounds. The level of hearing is compared with the person's level of hearing when the same sounds are played by way of speakers in the room. If the person hears the sounds at the same level by way of the ear and by way of the bone, the hearing problem is within the inner ear, because information is not passed to the brain. If the sound is heard more clearly by way of the bone than by way of the ear, it indicates that the inner ear is working properly and that the middle ear is failing to conduct sound waves to the inner ear.

This audiogram shows the hearing of a person with normal hearing. The blue line is the left ear, and the red is the right ear.

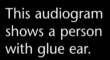

DEAFNESS

Deafness and hearing loss can affect people of any age. Some people are born deaf and never hear a sound throughout their lives. Some people begin to suffer hearing loss when they are young, while others only become deaf in old age. Whatever the cause and whatever the age, hearing loss and deafness can cause difficulties in everyday life.

Causes of hearing loss

Hearing loss can result from many things. The ears may be damaged by repeated exposure to very loud sounds or by an accident. Infections and other diseases may affect the ears and cause permanent damage. For example, if a pregnant woman becomes infected with rubella, her baby's ears may be damaged and may not develop properly. Some rare types of ear problems are hereditary.

Mild or severe?

Some people suffer only mild hearing loss. They may, for example, find it difficult to hear conversation if there is a lot of background noise, and they may need to turn up the volume on the television to hear it clearly. This level of hearing loss requires only minor changes to a person's lifestyle to allow for a normal life.

At the other end of the range are people who can hear absolutely nothing at all. They may need a lot of help and support to enable them to live independently.

Between these two extremes are many people who have a significant loss of hearing but, with some help, are able to live independent, active lives.

This audiogram shows a person with glue ear.

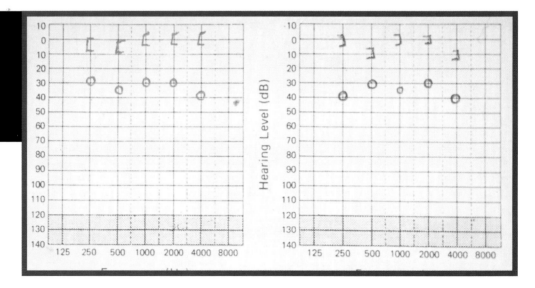

Restricted frequency range

Some people have a restricted **frequency** range that they can hear. For example, they may be able to hear low male voices clearly but struggle to pick up higher female voices. This restriction may be slight, with only a small, undetectable frequency range that causes few problems. However, if the range of frequencies a person can detect is very narrow, he or she may experience many problems.

This child is undergoing a hearing assessment. The sooner the hearing problems are detected and treated, the sooner he can begin to learn and develop his language skills.

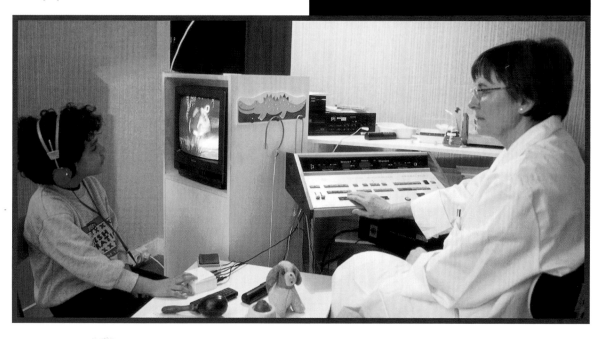

The age factor

Hearing plays a very important part in the learning process. As a baby, you heard the sound of your mother's voice and learned the familiar patterns of language from her and other people around you. You became used to everyday sounds and began to link them with events. For example, when the telephone rings, somebody picks up the receiver and speaks. Without this early learning, understanding everyday life is very difficult. The sooner a child's hearing loss is detected, assessed, and if possible, treated, the smaller its impact on his or her learning will be. Adults who lose their hearing have already usually completed their education so, although it may cause difficulties for them, it does not prevent them from achieving their potential.

Hearing problems and sports

People with hearing problems can take part in sports. Team sports, which often rely on reactions to a team member's call, may not be easy. However, many athletic events do not rely on the ability to hear, and individual sports, such as golf and swimming, are all possible.

Humans rely on being able to talk to each other. Without this, communication is difficult. Deaf people who cannot hear normal speech can communicate with each other and with people with normal hearing by using sign language.

The development of sign language

Centuries ago, in strict monasteries where monks were not allowed to talk to each other, systems of signs were used for communication. In the sixteenth century, an Italian doctor explored the possibilities of using a similar system to help deaf people. In 1620, the first book about teaching a sign language to deaf people was published.

The spread of sign language

In eighteenth-century Europe, several different systems of sign language developed, each corresponding to the spoken language of a particular country. An American, Thomas Hopkins Gallaudet, traveled to Europe and learned about the methods in use there. He founded the first school in the United States for deaf people. Others took up his ideas, and more schools and colleges for the deaf soon opened, all of which used sign language.

Use of sign language spread, allowing for communication between people who were deaf and those who could hear. Now in the United States, American Sign Language (ASL) is officially recognized as a foreign language. Qualifications in ASL are even accepted as part of the entry requirements to many colleges and universities.

These diagrams show the signs for each letter of the alphabet. Can you figure out how to spell your name or the town you live in?

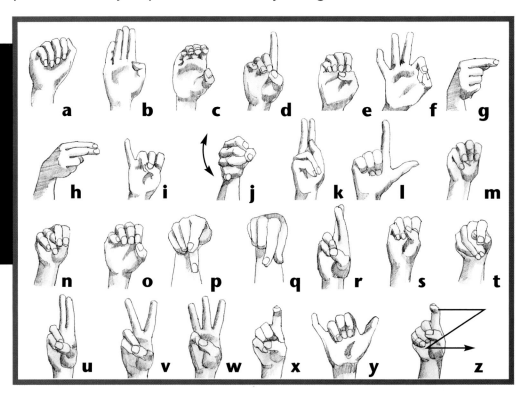

Sign language alphabet

Using the the American Manual Alphabet, you can make the signs that stand for each letter of the alphabet. With these, you can spell out a word or sentence that can be understood by anybody who reads sign language. This method is called finger spelling.

An alternative approach is that used by American Sign Language (ASL). In this language, signs are used to explain ideas rather than to spell out whole words. This is much quicker than spelling out individual words, conveying the meaning rather than exact sentences. For example, instead of spelling out "I have three dogs," an ASL user would make a sign for three, a sign for dog, and then point to himself or herself, saying "Three dogs, me."

0   1   2   3   4   5

6   7   8   9   10

Numbers have signs, too. You can use number signs one after another, for example, three followed by five means 35.

Using sign language

Many public meetings and conferences have an interpreter who stands on the stage or platform next to the speakers, in full view of the audience. The interpreter signs the words as they are spoken, allowing deaf people to participate and understand what is being said. News broadcasts on television also often have an interpreter, shown in a box on part of the screen.

This boy is learning sign language.

COPING WITH DEAFNESS

Deafness can make everyday tasks difficult, but with the right help and support, many problems can be overcome. Many devices are now available to help deaf and hard of hearing people, and as technology advances, new equipment is constantly being developed.

Communication

Hearing aids are used by many deaf people to help them to hear sounds around them. When you speak, your lips move to make the sounds of words. By watching these movements very carefully, you can figure out the sounds that the person is making. This is called lip reading. With practice, people can become very skilled at understanding speech in this way.

Videophones allow deaf people to communicate with each other. An ordinary telephone line is used, along with a computer or special video camera. When you dial the number and your call is answered, you and the person you have called can see a picture of each other. You can then have a conversation using sign language.

Everyday life

Many things around the home use sound to tell us things. The door bell rings, the telephone rings, the oven timer beeps. If you are deaf, all of these sounds are useless. Instead of sounds, these devices can

be fitted with lights so that a deaf person can see the signal instead of hearing it. Fire and smoke alarms can have special lighting effects so that a deaf person can be alerted to danger.

In addition, hearing dogs can be trained to respond to sounds. They are as important to people who are deaf as guide dogs are to people who are blind.

This videophone can help deaf people to communicate.

Subtitles for television programs and films allow people who are deaf to read a summary of what is being said. These allow them to follow a program or film in the same way that other people can use subtitles to follow a film in a foreign language.

There is no reason why people who are hard of hearing should not enjoy live music or theater. Many theaters and concert halls now have a hearing loop installed, allowing people with hearing impairments to experience the sounds of the performance.

Achieving success

In the past, deaf children were not expected to achieve very much. Today, however, people who are deaf are proving all the time that being deaf need not prevent anyone from being successful.

Marlee Matlin is a successful person who is deaf. She is an actress and has won many awards, including an Oscar for Best Actress. She has her own production company and makes television films.

Jack Ashley is an English politician. Despite being deaf, he has a successful political career and champions the rights of disabled people.

Evelyn Glennie is famous throughout the world as an outstanding percussionist. She has overcome her disability to achieve a highly successful career.

Evelyn Glennie

Evelyn Glennie is profoundly deaf, but despite this disability, she has become one of the greatest percussion players of her time. She gives solo performances at concert halls around the world, and her playing is admired and respected by musicians everywhere. Evelyn says that she feels different sounds in different parts of her body.

WHAT CAN GO WRONG WITH THE EARS?

This book has explained the different parts of the human ear, why they are important, and how they can be damaged by injury and illness. This page summarizes some of the problems that can affect people's ears. It also gives information about how each problem can be treated.

Many problems can be avoided by following healthy behaviors. This is called prevention. Getting regular exercise and plenty of rest are important, as is eating a balanced diet. This is especially important in your teenage years, when your body is still developing. The table here also tells you how you can prevent injury and illness to your ears.

Remember, if you think something is wrong with your body, you should always talk to a trained medical professional such as a doctor or your school nurse. Regular medical checkups are an important part of maintaining a healthy body.

Illness or injury	Cause	Symptoms	Prevention	Treatment
cauliflower ear	frequent **abrasion** and rubbing of the **pinna,** usually sport-related	lumpy, disfigured pinnae	wear a helmet or tape ears to the side of the head	plastic surgery may be possible for severe cases
ear infections	infection by **bacteria** or **viruses**	earache, pain, deafness, ringing noises in ear, possibly pus discharge	practice good personal hygiene; eat a healthy diet with plenty of fresh fruit and vegetables to provide vitamins needed for good health	depends on exact cause, but **antibiotics** may be used to treat bacterial infections
excess wax	buildup of excess wax in ear canal	reduced hearing in affected ear, irritation	practice good personal hygiene	wax softened with warm oil and then removed by doctor or nurse
stuck objects	object stuck in ear canal	hearing reduced in affected ear	Never put anything in your ear! Even cleaning the ear with tissues or cotton swabs can cause a problem.	careful removal of object by doctor or nurse

Illness or injury	Cause	Symptoms	Prevention	Treatment
deafness	many possible causes, but may be due to prolonged exposure to loud noises leading to damage to the **cochlea**	gradual deterioration in hearing	Keep personal stereos at low volume and avoid long periods of use. Wear protective ear muffs or ear plugs if working in noisy environment (or at a loud concert).	wearing a hearing aid may improve hearing

FURTHER READING

Basinger, Carol. *Everything You Need to Know about Deafness.* New York: Rosen, 2000.

Farndon, John. *Sound and Hearing.* Tarrytown, N.Y.: Marshall Cavendish, 2000.

Goode, Katherine. *Ears.* Detroit, Mich.: Gale Group, 2000.

Pringle, Laurence. *Hearing.* Tarrytown, N.Y.: Marshall Cavendish, 2000.

Sherman, Josepha. *The Ear: Learning How We Hear.* New York: Rosen, 2001.

GLOSSARY

abrasion damage caused by repeated rubbing

antibiotic drug used to fight infections. Antibiotics destroy microorganisms, such as bacteria or fungi, but are not effective against viruses.

anvil one of the tiny bones in the middle ear

audiologist person who carries out tests to find out how well people can hear

auditory nerve nerve that carries signals from the ear to the brain

bacterium microbe that can be useful or that can cause disease

basilar membrane membrane that lies beneath the hair cells of the spiral organ

cartilage strong, flexible material that protects bones

cochlea bony spiral in the inner ear

decongenstant medicine that reduces buildup of mucus

eardrum membrane that forms a barrier between the outer ear and the middle ear

eustachian tube tube connecting the middle ear and the upper part of the throat

frequency number of times something, such as sound waves, is repeated in a certain period of time

genetic having to do with passing characteristics from one generation to the next

hair cell cell with tiny hairs sticking out from its surface

hammer one of the tiny bones in the middle ear

inner ear fluid-filled innermost part of the ear

ligament strong cord that binds joints together

membrane thin layer of tissue

middle ear air-filled middle section of the ear

ossicle one of the three tiny bones of the middle ear

otolith granules that cover the surface of the otolithic membrane

otolithic membrane jellylike membrane that lies on top of the hair cells in the utriculus and saccule

oval window membrane that forms a partition between the middle ear and the inner ear

pinna flap of skin-covered cartilage that sticks out at the side of the head

pitch how high or low a sound is

radial fiber fine thread arranged like the spokes of a wheel

round window small, membrane-covered opening between the middle ear and inner ear, below the oval window

saccule part of the inner ear concerned with balance

semicircular canal one of three ducts in the inner ear that are concerned with balance

sound wave vibrations made by a sound source

spiral organ part of the inner ear that responds to vibrations

stirrup one of the tiny bones in the middle ear

tectorial membrane membrane that lies on top of hair cells in the spiral organ

utriculus part of the inner ear concerned with balance

virus microbe that uses the body's own cells to make copies of itself

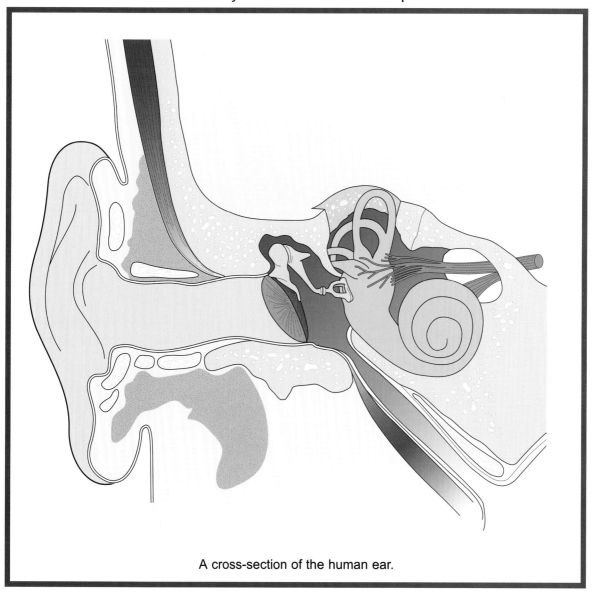

A cross-section of the human ear.

INDEX